Politics 101

The Unwritten Rules of Corporate Success

Frederick E. Darris II

Politics 101: The Unwritten Rules of Corporate Success

© 2025 Diversified Staffing Group. All rights reserved.

No part of this publication may be reproduced, stored in a retrieval system, or transmitted in any form or by any means (electronic, mechanical, photocopying, recording, or otherwise) without prior written permission from the author.

Published by Diversified Staffing Group

Surprise, Arizona

ISBN (Paperback): 979-8-9940140-0-4

Cover Design: Abdul Kalam

Interior Layout: Diversified Staffing Group

First Edition

Printed in the United States of America.

For more resources, visit: www.DivStaffing.com/DSGPlaybook

Contents

Preface 5
Introduction 9

1. People 13
2. Performance 17
3. Politics 22

Conclusion 27
Author's Note and Acknowledgments 29
About the Author 31

Preface

Every journey begins with a reason. Mine started with a simple but powerful question: *How do you succeed in a system that doesn't always play fair?*

From the wrestling mat to the corporate boardroom, I've learned that success isn't about luck; it's about discipline, preparation, and understanding the unwritten rules. My father showed me early on that the starting line isn't the same for everyone—and that I'd have to stay ready and stay sharp to stay ahead. My younger sister taught me fairness, the value of treating everyone with respect, no matter their background. And my mother taught me compassion, caring, and what it means to always find a way forward. Those lessons shaped how I carried myself long before I ever stepped into corporate America.

My brother taught me one of the earliest lessons that shaped my career: you have to believe it before you become it. He showed me that confidence starts on the inside long before the title shows up on the outside. Once you shift your mindset, your walk changes, your tone changes, and the room responds differently. That simple lesson guided how I approached sports, school, and eventually corporate America.

This book is for anyone who has ever felt overlooked, underestimated, or unsure of how to navigate the corporate game. It's for the professional who delivers results but still wonders why promotions pass them by. It's for the student preparing to enter the workforce, the entrepreneur building their own table, and the leader striving to leave a legacy.

The formula I share is not a theory.

Success = PEOPLE + performance + *Politics*

It's a lived experience. It's the reason I became the youngest Sloan Fellow in the program's worldwide history. It's the reason I thrived at General Motors, founded Diversified Staffing Group, and continue to mentor and empower others today.

I wrote this book because I believe success should be accessible. Too often, talented individuals fall short not because they lack ability, but because they don't understand the rules of the game. My goal is to pull back the curtain, to show you how relationships, execution, and influence work together to create opportunities.

If you take nothing else from these pages, remember this: success doesn't wait. Just like my coach told me on the mat, *"You wait, you get beat."* Don't wait for tomorrow. Don't wait for permission. Don't wait for someone else to hand you the opportunity. Step up, take the shot, and own your future.

This book is my gift to you; an invitation to move your mountain, one stone at a time, and to write a story of success that only you can author.

Now, in Chapter 1, we'll break down the formula for **Success = PEOPLE + performance + *Politics*,** showing how each part works in real life and why mastering the balance between them is the difference between simply surviving and truly leading.

Introduction

Success in Corporate America isn't random; it follows a formula. Over the course of my career, across industries and leadership roles, I discovered that thriving in the corporate world comes down to three elements: PEOPLE, performance, and *Politics*. Mastering the balance between them is the difference between simply surviving and truly leading.

This book, *Politics 101: The Unwritten Rules of Corporate Success*, is my way of sharing that formula with you. It's built on decades of lessons, many hard-earned, while some were passed down by mentors, and many were shaped by both challenges and triumphs. My goal is simple: to give you tools to navigate the system, elevate your career, and make your own "cover" look good.

From an early age, I was driven by fairness and justice. I was the student who stood up to bullies, the one who protected others. At home, my sister reinforced that principle—reminding me that fairness means showing equal respect to everyone, no matter their status or background. That principle of fairness became a cornerstone of how I approached relationships, leadership, and ultimately, success.

My journey has included moments that tested me deeply. When my youngest daughter passed away in 2021, my life was forever changed. Her memory reminds me daily of the importance of purpose, compassion, and perseverance. My oldest daughter continues to inspire me with her resilience and strength. Both have taught me lessons about love, patience, and legacy; lessons that shape how I lead, mentor, and live.

I am also the product of two powerful influences: my mother, who taught me compassion, caring, helping others, and always finding a way; and my father, a military man whose mantra—*"No excuse, sir"*—instilled in me discipline and accountability. Together, they built the foundation of my character.

Professionally, I've been blessed with milestones that shaped my perspective: serving as an executive at General Motors, founding Diversified Staffing Group, and earning advanced degrees from MIT, Lindenwood University, and the University of Missouri-Columbia.

The Sloan Fellows Program—established in 1930 by Alfred P. Sloan, then CEO of General Motors—is recognized as the world's first master's program for mid-career executives. It was designed to equip experienced leaders with advanced management, strategic, and global leadership skills. Over time, the program expanded to Stanford in 1957 and London Business School in 1968, producing alumni who have gone on to become Fortune 500 CEOs, Nobel laureates, and world leaders. Among its distinguished graduates are Kofi Annan, former Secretary-General of the United Nations and Nobel Peace Prize Laureate; Carly Fiorina, former CEO of Hewlett-Packard and the first woman to lead a Fortune top-20 company; and William Clay Ford Jr., current Executive Chairman of Ford Motor Company. Being named the youngest Sloan Fellow in the program's history was not only an honor but also a defining moment in my career, reinforcing the values of discipline, innovation, and leadership that continue to guide me today.

Athletics also played a defining role. Missouri State Champion in wrestling at 155 pounds, 1st Team All-State Middle Linebacker, and member of the 1985 Missouri Football State Championship Team. At the University of Missouri-Columbia, I wrestled in Division I at 150 pounds, ranking among the nation's top wrestlers. These experiences taught me resilience, teamwork, and the relentless pursuit of excellence, lessons that carried forward into every chapter of my professional life.

As Founder and President of Diversified Staffing Group (DSG), I dedicate my work to helping others "make their cover look good." Because the truth is, people do judge a book by its cover. My mission is to ensure that individuals and organizations not only look ready for opportunity but are truly prepared to seize it.

At DSG, we focus on two core missions: connecting companies with outstanding talent and coaching professionals to showcase their strengths in today's competitive job market. Whether it's building workforce solutions for organizations or empowering individuals through career tools and mentoring, DSG is about creating opportunities that elevate both people and businesses.

Here's the formula that drives this book and, I believe, corporate success itself:

- **30% PEOPLE** = who you know, who knows you, and the relationships you build;
- **30% performance** = the results you deliver and the standard you set; and
- **40% *Politics*** = the art of influence, managing perception, and building trust.

Put simply: **Success = PEOPLE + performance + Politics**

Each chapter will explore one of these components in depth, blending real stories with practical lessons. By the end, you'll not only understand the formula, you'll know how to apply it to your own career.

This book is my way of giving back to those who believed in me, to those who helped me along the way, and to those who are still finding their path. I hope that it encourages you to define your own success, discover your formula, and make your own cover look good.

Every opportunity I've ever had can be traced back to someone who took a risk on me and gave me a chance. Those moments of trust and belief shaped my path, and they remind me that success is never achieved alone. That's why the first part of the formula is PEOPLE is the foundation of everything else.

Chapter 1
PEOPLE

Every success story begins with PEOPLE. Every promotion, every opportunity, every breakthrough I've experienced can be traced back to relationships with mentors, colleagues, friends, and family who believed in me. That's why PEOPLE make up 30% of my success formula. Because no matter how talented or driven you are, success is never achieved in isolation. It's about who you know, how you connect, and how you nurture those relationships over time.

It's often said that we are only six degrees away from anyone in the world, creating a powerful reminder that opportunity is never far beyond our reach. The idea, known as "six degrees of separation," suggests that any two people on Earth are connected by a chain of no more than six acquaintances. In other words, through a series of "friend of a friend" connections, you could reach anyone—from a neighbor down the street to a world leader—within six steps. This principle highlights just how small and interconnected our world truly is, and why building relationships can open doors you never imagined.

In my experience, nearly every successful person has received help along the way. I'm no exception. During my time at General Motors, I had the support of almost two dozen mentors from departments across the company—Production, Maintenance, Engineering, Materials, Purchasing, and Finance, just to name a few. Whether I needed guidance on equipment installation, help navigating corporate procedures, or advice on problem-solving, there were always people willing to step up. These mentors were like the tutors I relied on during my electrical engineering studies at the University of Missouri-Columbia; they were knowledgeable, patient, and instrumental to my growth.

An automotive assembly plant is like a living organism, with each department serving as a vital organ that keeps the system running. Production drives the line's heartbeat, while Maintenance ensures the machinery and robotics never miss a beat. Plant Engineering designs the processes that enable efficiency, often guided by lean manufacturing principles. Quality safeguards every vehicle against flaws, while Materials and Purchasing keep the lifeblood of parts flowing. Human Resources manages the people who bring it all to life, and Finance ensures resources are allocated wisely and costs are controlled.

At the plant, the Body Shop builds the frame, the Paint Shop adds protection and finish, and Trim focuses on the vehicle's interior—seats, dashboards, and the details that make a car livable. The Chassis Department integrates the "brains and backbone" of the vehicle—engine, transmission, suspension, and steering systems—bringing structure and performance together. The Final Process team checks all the vehicle's functions, ensuring that everything from electronics to safety systems works as intended before the car leaves the line. Overseeing it all is the Safety Department, which ensures that every person and every process operates with discipline and care.

Together, these departments form an interconnected system—each one essential, each one dependent on the others—just like the formula for success itself:

Success = PEOPLE + performance + *Politics*

But the value of PEOPLE extends far beyond the workplace. My family and friends have been equally essential to my success. My mother and stepfather—whom I call Pops—have been pillars of support, as have my siblings and close friends. Their help came in many forms: financial, emotional, and intellectual. Whether I was bouncing ideas off them or leaning on them during tough times, they reminded me that success is rarely a solo effort. Independence is admirable, but interdependence is powerful.

Even before my high school success, my sister always had my back. Her example of fairness shaped how I saw people: beneath titles or circumstances, everyone deserves respect. She reminded me that regardless of someone's economic or social status, we all share the same need to be valued and heard. That lesson became a cornerstone of how I approach relationships in business and life, reinforcing that true leadership is built not on judgment or hierarchy, but on treating others with equal dignity.

That truth became even clearer as I ventured into entrepreneurship. Over the years, I've built and partnered in multiple businesses, learning that collaboration is key to scaling success. At MIT, one of the most valuable lessons I learned was to focus on my core strengths and outsource the rest. That principle became a foundation for my leadership style. For instance, while I was strong in math and technical analysis, I wasn't as passionate about accounting or finance. Instead of struggling through it, I partnered with people who thrived in those areas. By dividing responsibilities based on strengths, we were able to multiply results.

Lesson: Don't try to do everything yourself. Focus on your strengths and partner for the rest.

PEOPLE are the driving force behind every breakthrough, every promotion, and every success story. Whether it's forming strategic partnerships, seeking mentors who will challenge and guide you, or simply being open to learning from those around you, relationships matter. As the saying goes, *"It's not what you know, but who you know."* But I'd add one more layer: it's also who knows you and what you stand for. When people believe in your character, your integrity, and your drive, they become your advocates.

In essence, PEOPLE represent more than a percentage in my formula; it's the heart of success itself. Build authentic relationships, show appreciation for those who help you, and be willing to help others in return. Because at the end of the day, success isn't just about reaching the top; it's about who's there with you when you do.

But relationships alone won't carry you if you can't deliver. Connections may open the door, but only results will keep you in the room. To sustain credibility and earn continued opportunity, you must perform, which brings us to the next pillar of the formula: performance.

Chapter 2
performance

Performance is often the most visible measure of success. It accounts for 30% of my success formula and reflects not only what you do but also how far you're willing to go beyond what's expected. Hard work, dedication, and consistent execution form the foundation of great performance, but true excellence comes from the willingness to go the extra mile.

From an early age, my father taught me that in sports, and in life, you never want to leave your success in someone else's hands. His rule was simple: win by enough that nobody can take it from you. That philosophy shaped how I trained, studied, and later performed in corporate America. When the difference between you and the next person is small, decisions become subjective. But when the gap is wide, politics disappears. Performance speaks louder than preference.

Sports became my training ground for this lesson. In football, I was one of the smallest middle linebackers in the state of Missouri, at least by weight. But I made up for it by outworking everyone else. I studied our playbook until I knew it inside and out. I learned our opponents' game plan, their tendencies, and formations. On Mondays, when we watched film of the team we'd face that Friday, I wasn't just watching; I was memorizing. By game day, I knew what play was coming out of which formation, and that gave me a huge advantage.

That preparation leveled the playing field. I wasn't the biggest linebacker, but I was often the smartest one on the field. My edge came from discipline—hours of studying formations, recognizing patterns, and anticipating the opponent's play calls before they happened. That's where performance comes in: you can't control your size, but you can control how much you prepare.

Wrestling demanded the same mindset. Practice was never enough for me. I'd get up early to run and lose weight, practice after school, and run again at night. Back then, we didn't have the fancy gear wrestlers use today. We'd throw on plastic garbage bags underneath our gym clothes, turning every practice into a sauna just to cut weight. I worked out three times a day: before, during, and after practice: extra sit-ups, push-ups, leg lifts, and even extra runs. I mastered one unstoppable move on my feet, one move while on the bottom, and one move while on top—I did over a million drills. That's how I became a State Champion.

I had some big shoes to fill—my cousin was Mizzou's very first wrestling All-American. His success set the bar high and pushed me to train harder to prove I could carry on that legacy. When I wrestled Division I in college, the grind only intensified—running before class, wrestling after class, and conditioning again at night. Cutting weight, riding the stationary bike, endless sprawl drills, hand-fighting conditioning, and jumping rope. You had to bust your butt every single day just to keep up, let alone get ahead.

That same work ethic carried into my professional life. At General Motors, even as an intern, I made sure I was the first one in and the last one out. If everyone started at 7:00 a.m., I was there at 6:31 a.m. If everyone left at 4:00 p.m., I stayed until 5:00 p.m. When I became full-time, I pushed even harder—seven days a week, twelve to fourteen hours a day, not for overtime pay but to expand my knowledge. I learned every department: Plant Engineering, Production, Maintenance, Materials, Body Shop, Paint Shop, Trim, Chassis, and Final Process. One of my mentors, the plant manager, told me, *"Learn every position in this plant as if you're going to run it one day."* So, I did.

Lesson: performance means putting in the extra work before, during, and after everyone else.

Even the greats had to do it. Tom Brady wasn't the strongest, fastest, or most gifted quarterback when he entered the NFL. But he studied harder than anyone. He knew defenses, players' strengths and weaknesses, and his own teammates' tendencies. He could audible at the line of scrimmage, calling a different play than initially planned in the huddle if he saw something in the defense. That kind of preparation allowed him to anticipate nearly every possible scenario and adjust in real time. That's why he performed at such a high level for so long, because he worked harder than anyone else.

I'll never forget a wrestling match in college against an All-American—one of the top eight wrestlers in the nation. I was losing, down by one point, with less than 31 seconds left. If I took him down, I would win. But I hesitated. After the match, my coach lit into me: "Darris, why didn't you shoot?" I told him I was waiting for the right opportunity. He looked me dead in the eye and said, "You wait...you get beat. You hear me, Darris? You wait...you f---ing get beat!"

That stuck with me forever. Just like in the *Rocky* movies, *"There is no tomorrow!"* That phrase has echoed in my head ever since. Performance means you don't wait. You act. You push. You take the shot.

Academics demanded the same discipline. At MIT, I saw the principle play out in real time. Typically, professors assign reading before classes start. But on my very first day, a professor didn't. Instead of giving us a break, he added three more chapters to read over the weekend, due Monday. That was my "welcome to MIT" moment. I often worked until two in the morning, balancing ambition with the need for rest.

But preparation had always been my edge. I earned a full-ride academic scholarship, proof that discipline in the classroom mattered just as much as discipline on the mat or field. I learned quickly that professors notice effort. I sat in the front of my college classes, took detailed notes, and even learned professors' hobbies, the ages of their kids, and what kept them up at night. Professors liked watching me write down the "important things" they said, even if sometimes it was my to-do list or grocery list, because running out of food was a no-no. That attention to detail built trust and credibility, giving me an edge that others overlooked.

When I mentor younger professionals or student athletes, I ask a simple question: "What did you do today to get closer to your goal?" But I don't stop there. What did you do yesterday? What did you do this past weekend? Because how bad do you really want it? Your competition practiced all last week, this past weekend, yesterday, and is working out right now as we speak.

I tell people this all the time: you don't become a 3x State Champion (once in wrestling and twice in football) if you're not willing to work three times harder than the next person. That's the price of excellence.

Many have dreams of becoming athletes, executives, or entrepreneurs, but far fewer are willing to outwork everyone else to make it happen. Michael Jordan didn't become the best by talent alone; he practiced late into the night. Tiger Woods didn't dominate golf by luck; he hit thousands of balls long after others went home. Success demands that kind of obsession and consistency.

In college wrestling, repetition was everything. Our coach drilled us relentlessly—move after move, day after day—until technique became instinct. That repetition built confidence and muscle memory under pressure, a principle that applies equally in business. The more you practice excellence, the more naturally it becomes part of who you are.

Lesson: If you're behind, you can't just keep pace, you must accelerate. Like driving at 65 mph to catch someone going 55, success requires extra effort to close the gap and surpass the competition.

So, how bad do you want it? That question defines performance. Because in the end, performance isn't just about showing up; it's about showing out, delivering beyond expectations, and setting a standard that others aspire to reach.

But even the best performers can be overlooked if they ignore the other parts of the formula. Relationships open doors, performance keeps you in the room; but *Politics* determines how far you rise. That's where we turn next.

Chapter 3
Politics

Politics represents the largest portion of my success formula at 40%. If performance is about proving you belong, *Politics* is about determining how far you'll go once you're in the room. It's the difference between being noticed and being chosen, between being considered and being promoted.

The key to *Politics* is simple: get people to like you. Once they like you, they will surely go out of their way to help you. When people like you, it's that much harder to tell you no. Think about it: you just spent an hour in the car with your friend since grade school…who are you going to pick when it's time to choose teams? Familiarity and trust almost always win.

But here's the catch: don't hate the player, hate the game. If you want to change the outcome, you need influence. That means having the ear of someone sitting at the table, because those around the table make decisions. Or better yet, get to the table yourself. Get promoted so you're one of the decision makers. And the ultimate step? Run the meeting. Be the head of the table.

At its core, *Politics* is about trust, not titles. People naturally lean toward those who feel familiar—those they've worked with, spent time with, or built real rapport with. Think about choosing teams for a pickup basketball game. You might have a slightly better player nearby, but you'll usually pick your longtime friend who rode with you to the gym. It's not bias; it's comfort and trust. The same thing happens in business: when the differences between people are small, relationships become the deciding factor.

But talent can override familiarity. If someone's ability is far superior—think LeBron James—you'll pick them without hesitation. My father used to tell me, "Win so decisively they can't take it from you." That lesson applies to corporate life, too. When performance differences are small, relationships determine outcomes. But when your skill and value are undeniable, people have no choice but to pick you.

One of my mentors once told me, "Kiss the ring, but don't go below the belt." That phrase stuck with me. In *Politics*, you have to show respect to supervisors, managers, and upper leadership. You play nice, but you don't sell your soul. You can be humble without being a pushover, respectful without being submissive. That balance—respect with integrity—is the essence of political savvy.

I learned early that in politics, appearances aren't cosmetic, they're strategic. It taught me that leadership is often communicated before a word is spoken. I studied executives closely. I noticed how they wore jackets into meetings or onto the plant floor, then took them off during discussions as if to roll up their sleeves and work alongside employees. But when they left, the jacket went back on. It was a subtle signal of authority and approachability.

I paid attention to how they greeted people—always with a confident "Good morning" and a quick "Good...Good" when asked how they were doing. I studied how they walked: head up, shoulders back, moving with pride and presence, whether in the corporate office or on the assembly floor. Even in the plant, you could spot the executives by their jackets, their stride, and their tone. *Politics* is about those details—how you walk, how you talk, how you carry yourself—because people are often judging the cover before they read the book.

I also noticed the small things, like how people left voicemail messages. They did so with confidence and repeated the important details. When leaving your phone number on an answering machine, talk slowly as if someone is writing it down, and repeat the last four digits in two different forms: *"3-4-2-5...that's thirty-four twenty-five."* Those little touches build clarity and credibility.

Lesson: Politics is not about manipulation; it's about connection. Shared experiences and polished presence build trust faster than formal meetings ever could.

For me, golf became one of those shared experiences. Golf isn't just a sport; it's a five-hour conversation. Unlike a short coffee meeting, a round of golf offers hours of relaxed interaction, giving both parties the chance to build trust and truly get to know each other. On the course, guards drop, personalities emerge, and authentic bonds form. That's why golf has become such an important part of doing business in corporate America. If I knew then what I know now, I would have started golfing much earlier in my career.

In business, you often fight just to get a fifteen or twenty-minute meeting with someone to market your ideas or pitch your company. Golf changes that dynamic. Instead of rushing through a presentation in a boardroom, you're outdoors, in nature, spending hours together in a relaxed environment. That extended time allows conversations to flow naturally, alliances to solidify, and trust to build in ways that a quick meeting never could. And when the round ends, you often share another hour over food and drinks—cementing the connection even further.

I don't just play; I compete. I'm a 3x Club Champion at The Wyndgate Country Club in Michigan (Senior Division, 1st Flight, and 2nd Flight)...but who's counting. Those victories weren't just about trophies; they were about discipline, preparation, and consistency, the same traits that drive success in business and leadership. Sometimes it came down to the smallest margin, such as having to two-putt to win a championship. Whether it's sinking that putt under pressure or delivering results in a high-stakes meeting, success comes down to staying calm, focused, and confident when the spotlight is brightest.

But golf isn't the only way to connect. I've found that playing Texas Hold'em, chess, or knowing a little about each major sport can instantly build rapport. Find something in common with someone, and all of a sudden, they like you. *Politics* is about finding those bridges, those shared interests, that make people feel comfortable and connected.

Travel also expanded my political awareness. I've taken international trips to Asia—China, Japan, South Korea—visited Brazil, Mexico, Germany, and countries throughout Europe, and traveled through 31 states in the United States. Experiencing cultures in different countries helped me avoid prejudging others who look, think, and act differently than I do. It taught me that beneath the surface, people everywhere share the same desire for respect, opportunity, and connection.

Those experiences reinforced that *Politics* isn't just corporate; it's cultural. Every country, every community has its own unwritten rules, and the more you understand them, the more adaptable and likable you become.

I'm also a firm believer in the Law of Attraction. Whatever you think about consistently has a way of showing up in your life. Negative thoughts attract negative outcomes; positive thoughts attract positive ones.

That belief started with my brother. In high school, he told me, "You just have to believe it. You have to think it, act it, and play like you're the best." He taught me to step into the role mentally before I ever held it physically. Years later, I realized that mindset was the *Politics* of the mind, because when you believe it, act it, and carry yourself with confidence, others begin to see you that way too. Eventually, the vision becomes reality.

Here's another truth: influence isn't just about where you sit, it's about what you build. Real change happens when you stop waiting for permission and start shaping the space yourself. To make a difference, you need more than presence; you need the power to set the agenda, guide the conversation, and drive decisions. That's how influence works in corporate *Politics*.

But there's one step beyond even that: entrepreneurship. Because when you build your own business, you don't just sit at the table; you own the table. You set the agenda, you decide who gets invited, and you create opportunities not only for yourself but for others. Entrepreneurship is the ultimate goal, the point where PEOPLE, performance, and *Politics* converge into independence and impact. It's where you stop playing someone else's game and start designing your own.

Small things make a big difference too: smile often, dress neatly, smell good, and maintain fresh breath. People enjoy being around those who radiate positive energy. When you exude enthusiasm, confidence, and optimism, others naturally want to be around you and help you succeed.

Ultimately, mastering corporate *Politics* isn't about playing games; it's about building trust, showing respect, and becoming someone others genuinely want to support.

Conclusion

In the end, the formula for success in corporate America, as outlined in *Politics 101: The Unwritten Rules of Corporate Success*, is both deliberate and straightforward: **Success = PEOPLE + performance + *Politics*.** Each element is essential, and true success requires balance among all three. Excelling in only two areas isn't enough. If you master PEOPLE and performance but ignore *Politics*, you'll reach only part of your potential. Likewise, focusing solely on *Politics* and PEOPLE without delivering results leaves you short. To reach your full potential, you must integrate all three.

Think of it this way: achieving 25% in PEOPLE, 25% in performance, and 35% in *Politics* gives you an 85% success rate, which is an impressive score that demonstrates the power of balance. The key is to develop relationships, execute at a high level, and navigate the political landscape with both strategy and integrity. When these components align, your opportunities multiply, and your influence expands.

I'm profoundly grateful to everyone who has supported me along this journey, especially my family, friends, mentors, business partners, clients, and customers. And to my employees, both past and present: thank you. Your dedication, effort, and belief in the mission have been the backbone of every success I've achieved. Without you, none of this would be possible.

Above all, I give praise to God Almighty. *To God be the glory.* Every opportunity, every lesson, and every victory has been guided by His hand. My faith has carried me through challenges and triumphs alike, and it remains the foundation of my purpose.

This book represents my attempt to give back, to share the lessons, principles, and faith that have carried me through a lifetime of challenges and triumphs. I hope that the ideas here not only inform you but inspire you to act, to lead, and to build your own path to success through PEOPLE, performance, and *Politics*.

And remember, how do you move a mountain? One stone at a time. Success is built through consistent effort, day after day, choice after choice.

We've talked about taking the shot before, but it bears repeating: success doesn't wait. One of the first lessons I learned on the mat was simple, hesitation loses. The longer you pause, the faster someone else moves. Don't wait for tomorrow. Don't wait for permission. Don't wait for someone else to hand you the opportunity. Step up, take the shot, and own your future.

Author's Note and Acknowledgments

Writing *Politics 101: The Unwritten Rules of Corporate Success* has been both humbling and rewarding. While this is my first published book outside of my thesis at MIT, it represents far more than words on a page; it represents the people, experiences, and lessons that have shaped my life and career.

First and foremost, I give praise to God Almighty. *To God be the glory.* Every opportunity, every lesson, and every victory has been guided by His hand. My faith has carried me through challenges and triumphs alike, and it remains the foundation of my purpose.

To my family, you have been my foundation. My mother and father instilled in me discipline, compassion, and resilience. My sister taught me fairness and the importance of treating everyone the same, regardless of background. My daughters remind me daily of purpose, love, and legacy.

To my late brother, you gave me one of the earliest and most powerful lessons in the Law of Attraction: to think, act, and carry myself as if I already was the person or position I aspired to become. That wisdom shaped my confidence on the field, on the mat, and later in the boardroom. Though you're no longer here, the belief you placed in me continues to echo through my journey, reminding me that vision backed by conviction eventually becomes reality. Your influence lives on in every chapter of this book and in every step I take, a lasting testament to the love, guidance, and faith you poured into me.

To my siblings and extended family, your encouragement has been a constant source of fuel.

To my mentors and colleagues: you opened doors, shared wisdom, and challenged me to grow. From the shop floor to the executive suite, your guidance has left an unforgettable mark on my journey.

To my business partners, customers, and especially my clients, thank you for trusting me, for allowing me to serve, and for inspiring me with your own stories of perseverance and success. You are the reason I continue to push forward, innovate, and give back.

To my employees—both past and present—thank you. Your dedication, effort, and belief in the mission have been the backbone of every success I've achieved. Without you, none of this would be possible.

To my friends: you celebrated the wins, steadied me through the setbacks, and reminded me to laugh along the way.

And finally, to the reader, thank you for investing your time in these pages. I hope that this book serves as both a guide and a spark, helping you navigate your own path with confidence, courage, and clarity.

This is not the end of the journey; it's just another beginning. May you take these principles, apply them with purpose, and write a story of success that is uniquely your own.

About the Author

Frederick E. Darris II is a strategist, mentor, and entrepreneur. As a former General Motors Executive and the youngest Sloan Fellow in program history, he built a career shaped by the principles he teaches in this book: PEOPLE, performance, & *Politics*.

Before entering corporate leadership, Fred excelled as a nationally ranked Division I College Wrestler, a State Champion in both wrestling and football, and a 3x Club Champion at The Wyndgate Country Club (Senior Champion, 1st Flight Champion, and 2nd Flight Champion). His athletic achievements reflect the discipline, resilience, and competitive drive he brings into every area of his life.

Today, Fred serves as Founder & President of Diversified Staffing Group (DSG), where he helps companies find great people and empowers professionals to showcase their strengths. He credits every success to God Almighty. To God be the glory.

When he's not building businesses or mentoring professionals, Fred enjoys family time, golf, Texas Hold'em, and studying the habits of high performers. His mission is simple: to help others define their formula for success—**Success = PEOPLE + performance + *Politics***—and leverage it to build a legacy of opportunity.

www.ingramcontent.com/pod-product-compliance
Lightning Source LLC
Chambersburg PA
CBHW070952180426
43194CB00042B/2477